American
Station Wagons

The Golden Era 1950-1975

Those were the days ... ™

VELOCE

Other great books from Veloce –

Those Were The Days ... Series
Alpine Trials & Rallies 1910-1973 (Pfundner)
American 'Independent' Automakers – AMC to Willys 1945 to 1960 (Mort)
American Station Wagons – The Golden Era 1950-1975 (Mort)
American Trucks of the 1950s (Mort)
American Trucks of the 1960s (Mort)
American Woodies 1928-1953 (Mort)
Anglo-American Cars from the 1930s to the 1970s (Mort)
Austerity Motoring (Bobbitt)
Austins, The last real (Peck)
Brighton National Speed Trials (Gardiner)
British Lorries of the 1950s (Bobbitt)
British Lorries of the 1960s (Bobbitt)
British Touring Car Racing (Collins)
British Police Cars (Walker)
British Woodies (Peck)
Café Racer Phenomenon, The (Walker)
Drag Bike Racing in Britain – From the mid '60s to the mid '80s (Lee)
Dune Buggy Phenomenon, The (Hale)
Dune Buggy Phenomenon Volume 2, The (Hale)
Endurance Racing at Silverstone in the 1970s & 1980s (Parker)
Hot Rod & Stock Car Racing in Britain in the 1980s (Neil)
Last Real Austins 1946-1959, The (Peck)
MG's Abingdon Factory (Moylan)
Motor Racing at Brands Hatch in the Seventies (Parker)
Motor Racing at Brands Hatch in the Eighties (Parker)
Motor Racing at Crystal Palace (Collins)
Motor Racing at Goodwood in the Sixties (Gardiner)
Motor Racing at Nassau in the 1950s & 1960s (O'Neil)
Motor Racing at Oulton Park in the 1960s (McFadyen)
Motor Racing at Oulton Park in the 1970s (McFadyen)
Superprix – The Story of Birmingham Motor Race (Page & Collins)
Three Wheelers (Bobbitt)

From Veloce Publishing's new imprints:

Battle Cry!
Soviet General & field rank officer uniforms: 1955 to 1991 (Streather)
Red & Soviet military & paramilitary services: female uniforms 1941-1991 (Streather)

Hubble & Hattie
Complete Dog Massage Manual, The – Gentle Dog Care (Robertson)
Dinner with Rover (Paton-Ayre)
Dog cookies (Schops)
Dog Games – stimulating play to entertain your dog and you (Blenski)
Dog Relax – Relaxed dogs, relaxed owners (Pilguj)
Excercising your puppy: a gentle & natural approach (Robertson)
Know your dog – The guide to a beautiful relationship (Birmelin)
Living with an older dog (Alderton & Hall)
My dog has cruciate ligament injury (Haüsler & Friedrich)
My dog is blind – but lives life to the full! (Horsky)
My dog is deaf (Willms)
My dog has hip dysplasia (Haüsler & Friedrich)
Motorway walks (Rees)
Smellorama – nose games for dogs (Theby)
Swim to recovery – canine hydrotherapy healing (Wong)
Waggy tails & wheelchairs (Epp)
Winston ... the dog who changed my life (Klute)
You and your Border Terrier – The Essential Guide (Alderton)
You and your Cockapoo – The Essential Guide (Alderton)

First published in September 2010 by Veloce Publishing Limited, Veloce House, Parkway Farm Business Park, Middle Farm Way, Poundbury, Dorchester, Dorset, DT1 3AR, England.
Fax 01305 250479/e-mail info@veloce.co.uk/web www.veloce.co.uk or www.velocebooks.com.
ISBN: 978-1-845842-68-0 UPC: 6-36847-04268-4
Readers with ideas for automotive books, or books on other transport or related hobby subjects, are invited to write to the editorial director of Veloce Publishing at the above address.
British Library Cataloguing in Publication Data – A catalogue record for this book is available from the British Library. Typesetting, design and page make-up all by Veloce Publishing Ltd on Apple Mac.
Printed in India by Replika Press.

Contents

Preface

This is the seventh book that I have written in conjunction with my son, Andrew. His photographic skills help illustrate the often flamboyant and unique styling of the American station wagon, as well as the many practical and convenience features developed over the years, intended to capture the attention of prospective buyers. These dual-purpose work and family wagon designs built by American automakers following WWII were unique in their wide range of models, sizes and design. Few American children grew up in this era without having at least a ride in an American-built station wagon. Today, it is this 'connection' that makes these unique people and cargo transporters appealing to a dedicated group of collectors and enthusiasts.

As well as my enthusiasm and fascination with these American vehicles, and Andrew's photographic talents, this book would not have been possible without the encouragement, kindness and co-operation of many others.

Some of the advertisement and brochure images were provided courtesy of Norm McWaters and Thomas McPherson. The rare 1956 Studebaker President Pinehurst station wagon is owned by Normand Gautreau. Other enthusiasts who provided photos of their wagons include Fred Dol (1966 Dodge Dart), Dave Cleveland (1957 Pontiac), Ross Wooldridge (1966 Chrysler), Wes Ball (1954 Chrysler), Howard Furtak (1958 Pontiac), Peter Preuss (1963 Chev), and Chris Whillans for his two Nash Statesman sedans.

Hyman Motors Ltd, kindly supplied numerous images, as did Legendary Motor Car Ltd and The Stable Ltd.

Andrew and I would also like to thank Rod Grainger of Veloce Publishing.

Introduction

The term 'station wagon' was the more modern name for the 'depot hack' that had emerged in the 1920s. Very often, these early wagons or hacks were seen at train stations across North America, picking up passengers and their luggage, and transporting them home or to an hotel or inn. The depot hack was originally based on a touring car chassis, with a spacious wooden body constructed to fit from the cowl back. Some small truck chassis were also utilized by fitting a hack body, along with rear seats and an extended roof.

As closed cars became the norm by the end of the 1920s, sedan models were usually converted for station wagon use by removing the enclosed bodywork from the front cowl back. In the later thirties, the now all-steel body sedans were still used, but continued to be custom-built with a wooden wagon body for the limited station wagon market.

Following WWII most American manufacturers continued to offer 'woody' wagons, yet it soon became obvious that continuing development of interstate highways and better roads was resulting in a dramatic decline in the number of passengers travelling by train.

The first real station wagons are usually accredited to the Ford Motor Company, which began building them soon after the Model A was introduced in 1928. Pictured is a 1929 Model A Ford 'Woody' from a company brochure. (Author's collection)

By 1957 color comics were popular nationwide, and so, like others, AMC Rambler adopted the concept in its advertising. William Steig, creator of this comic, was a highly successful illustrator and cartoonist, and would go on (starting in the 1960s) to write over thirty children's books, including *Shrek*, the basis of four highly acclaimed films. (Author's collection)

The new, post-war prosperity was allowing more people to get behind the wheel of their own vehicle, and the station wagon's role in American life was changing as a result.

5

This 1956 Studebaker Pinehurst is the epitome of American station wagons of the fifties, with its two-tone paint, lots of glittering chrome, and smooth-running eight-cylinder engine. (Andrew Mort)

At the same time, Americans were moving to the burgeoning suburbs and commuting to work. Gasoline was inexpensive and more families were buying two cars, as public transportation to and from the suburbs or satellite towns lagged well behind the building boom in housing developments. Driving to holiday and resort locations was much easier now, and, as a result, there was a growing demand for functional designs to carry luggage, camping and fishing gear, and haul boats and trailers for longer distances.

Camping was becoming popular for family holidays, which meant either hauling a tent, or sleeping in or by the car.

For most American families, the traditional wooden station wagon cost too much to buy and maintain. At the same time, American car manufacturers in the highly competitive post-war marketplace were discovering that building a 'woody' wagon didn't justify the limited production and costs. In most cases, the off-site specialist firms building these vehicles were constructing essentially coachbuilt bodies.

The first all-steel station wagons began to appear after WWII, with the 1946 Willys Jeep-based version one of the first. Other manufacturers followed suit, and some – like Pontiac – even offered a real woody wagon *and* an almost identical, all-steel, painted, faux woody in 1949.

By the 1960s, station wagons were becoming more and more flamboyant, and featured distinctive styling cues and trim very often not seen on the rest of the model range. This is a 1962 Oldsmobile Fiesta station wagon, with additional trim added by its owner. (Andrew Mort)

The station wagon was evolving and steady sales showed both 'baby boomer' families and businesses liked the extra seating and storage capacity, with none of the utilitarian style and passenger restrictions of the popular American sedan and pickup. There was little it couldn't handle, yet still provided the same performance, comfort and safety of a sedan. And, while the station wagon nomenclature remained, it was becoming the 'station' that people wanted to attain.

At the start of the 1950s, the station wagon market accounted for around three per cent of domestic sales, and by 1960 that figure had increased to over fifteen per cent.

Nearly every American car manufacturer entered the market, except for luxury marques such as Cadillac and Lincoln. Smaller, struggling independents often competed in this market by providing station wagon space and convenience in creatively-designed sedans.

As the decade continued, station wagons began to appear in the compact, intermediate and full-size line-ups of the surviving four major American automotive producers, in a range that was extensive, and which could be luxuriously trimmed or purchased as low-priced, entry level models.

Luxuries often included a more powerful V8, but for those seeking the best fuel economy, a larger, six-cylinder model could be trimmed out at a high level.

In America at that time it was a case of 'bigger is better,' so a wide choice of V8 engines was always on offer, together with rarer dealer or special factory options, if required: four-door and two-door wagons – based on hardtop and sedan models – were also offered.

American station wagons of the 1950s and early 1960s featured lots of pizzazz, as well as utility. And, no matter how many years had passed since the disappearance of real wood, many buyers opted to have their station wagon with woodgrain appliqué.

Along with development of the all-steel station wagon came a new era and a fresh perspective, which redefined the role of this utilitarian vehicle in American society.

A people and cargo transporter with towing capacity; Americans with more leisure time were on the road and seeing America – and what better way to do it, than in a station wagon?

Due to space restrictions, it's not been possible to feature all of the station wagons built in America over the quarter century that this book covers. In some cases, we have focused on lesser known makes and models in order to better capture and demonstrate the style and design of the period. Overall, we have tried to illustrate the wide variety of models available when the wagon was both family standard and status symbol of a successful American lifestyle.

Norm and Andrew Mort

1945-1949: The age of change

Prior to WWII the station wagon was a niche market, where sales could be made relatively easily, yet construction of an all-wood station wagon body was labour intensive, and thus expensive to build.

War production brought with it improved methods and technology, and after WWII all the American car manufacturers moved away from separate frame and body construction to unibody station wagon designs, and the use of real wood soon ceased. By the beginning of the 1950s, even wood trim inside and out on stylish convertibles, sedans and station wagons was disappearing. The Willys Jeep-based station wagon appeared in 1946, and is considered the first all-steel, production station wagon built in volume.

Ford, the largest manufacturer of 'Woody' station wagons, halted production in 1948. Its first, all-new-Ford line-up would include a steel wagon, but with some plywood molding and paneling.

The Willys Jeep-based station wagon was one of the first all-steel wagons to be built, and proved a popular model. Its very straight, flat side panels were horizontally and vertically ribbed for added strength, but also gave it a typical 'Woody' look, though without the lumber. Kaiser – seeking another car line to replace the Frazer (1946-1951) – purchased Willys in 1953, providing Kaiser dealers with their first station wagon in the process. (Author's collection)

Larger and more truck-like than a station wagon, this 1935 Chevrolet 'Carry-All' featured a steel body in an age when station wagons had virtually custom-built wooden bodies. Originally, 'Carry-Alls' tended to feature a single opening rear door, but soon dual doors, or split doors with a tailgate were offered to assist loading.

During this period the term 'Suburban' was also used by various manufacturers for their 'Carry-Alls' and station wagon models well into the 1960s, before the name ultimately became the property of General Motors in May 1988. (Author's collection)

New 'Hydra-Coil' Springs

Ford's first all-new post-war design in 1949 was awarded a 'Fashion Medal,' and included a two-door steel station wagon. The age of the 'Woody' station wagon was quickly drawing to a close, and a four-door version was no longer available. The wood trim on this new wagon was purely decorative, and had gone by 1952, in any case. Ford built 31,412 wagons in 1949, compared to just 8912 in 1948. (Author's collection)

The Packard Motor Car Company's last real station wagon was typical of the transitional design from wood to all-steel, despite being adorned with northern birch trim and painted woodgrain panels, none of which was structural, but simply decoration for the steel body. Known by Packard as its 'Standard Station Sedan,' it was not a 'DeLuxe' model, but part of the 'Standard Eight' series, so therefore fitted with the smaller straight eight. Weighing in at 4075lb (1848kg), it cost the stately sum of $3450.00US. Production ceased in 1950. (Author's collection)

NEW CROSLEY SUPER MODELS

with roll-down windows and special deluxe features

See – drive the newest, smartest Crosley Cars – the new SUPER CROSLEY in all passenger models. Each one has major improvements inside and out. Yet all retain the Crosley proved economy. Low down payment. Low monthly payments. Up to 50 miles on a gallon of regular gasoline. Super models are an addition and do not replace the standard line.

The 1948 Crosley models – including station wagons – were the first American cars equipped with four-wheel disc brakes. To further enhance sales potential, the interior was dressed in a bright, colorful, long-wearing plastic-coated material. The Crosley brochure pointed-out it was "... a practical, roomy wagon with a removable rear seat that allowed for enough space for a quarter ton load with two huskies riding in the front." (Author's collection)

In fact, most of the all-new, post-war American station wagons were steel, unibody designs. The only real wood still used was the inside and outside trim, or the loading floor. The fabricated wood look was paint, plastic, or a paper appliqué known as 'Dinoc,' developed by 3M In 1949.

Plymouth led the way in offering a low priced, all-steel station wagon, yet, in 1948, prestigious Packard introduced a 'Woody' clad station wagon, within its all-new line-up, in trying to compete with Ford, GM, and Chrysler. It was Packard's first station wagon since 1941.

Over the years Buick had become recognized as the leading maker of luxurious station wagons, and in 1953 was the last American manufacturer to build a traditional 'Woody' wagon.

Both Chevrolet and Oldsmobile offered station wagons in wood, and then steel, well before that, whilst Pontiac offered its wagon in these materials in 1949.

However, as the 1940s were drawing to a close, the largest producer of station wagons in America was Crosley – one of the smallest independent American automakers – which produced a micro-sized wagon.

Powel Crosley Jr had been immensely successful in virtually every financial endeavour he took on, and by 1922 Crosley was the world's largest manufacturer of radios. After breaking into radio broadcasting, Crosley next ventured into building kitchen appliances, and owned the patent for shelves in refrigerator doors. Yet, he still wanted to fulfill his boyhood dream of building automobiles. On April 29th, 1939, at the Indianapolis Speedway, Crosley introduced his microcar-sized 'Car of Tomorrow,' priced at just over $300; powered by a four-cylinder engine built by the Waukesha Motor Company, and sold through his 200 Crosley dealers – or any store that carried the company's appliances.

Sales were slow initially, with a mere 442 units built in 1940. With an improved powertrain, production rose to 2289 units in 1941, and had reached over 1000 in 1942 before manufacture was halted.

Following WWII, Crosley introduced new post-war models powered by a 26.5hp, 44cu in (721cc), copper-brazed Cobra, four-cylinder engine, and with fresh styling. To begin with, only a sedan was offered, but a convertible and a pickup were added as the first post-war sales year ended. Initially slow sellers, total production in 1947 exceeded 19,000, and rose to 28,734 in 1948, which included 23,489 station wagons. That total made Crosley America's – and the world's – largest producer of station wagons.

The Crosley plant was then expanded by 40 per cent, but engine defects, combined with an increasing number of full-size, secondhand cars, resulted in a dramatic decline in sales. For 1949, a new engine was designed and installed in yet another re-styled model line-up; despite this, production plunged to just 7431 units, of which only 3803 were station wagons. Production continued to decline, and was halted in 1952.

Crosley stated unashamedly in its brochure: "Look at the sweeping lines of the new Crosley Station Wagon, a triumph of designing by Crosley, the world's largest producer of station wagons." Crosley models ranged in weight from 1175 to 1403lb (533-636kg), while prices ranged downward from the top-of-the-line station wagon at only $929US FOB Marion, Indiana. (Author's collection)

As well as station wagons, American manufacturers built Carry-Alls, larger vehicles usually built on a truck chassis, which were really a multi-passenger version of an American panel truck, but with glass windows instead of metal panels. The result was a vehicle the size and power of a truck with the seating of a station wagon. One of the first models was the all-steel Carry-All, built by Chevrolet in 1935, and based on its small panel delivery truck chassis.

In most cases, the 'Carry-All' and 'Suburban' names were applied to a station wagon-like vehicle built on a commercial chassis, though not exclusively. DeSoto built a Carry-All in 1949, based on its limousine model. Plymouth, as well as Chevrolet and others, built station wagon models referred to as the 'Suburban'; while, in 1950-51, DeSoto built a Frazer Vagabond-like model known as the 'Carry-All.'

Regardless of what name it carried, as the decade ended, the popularity of the American station wagon was about to explode ...

It looks like a station wagon, hauls like a station wagon, and has enough seats for a family – so it must *be* a station wagon! No? Then, when is a station wagon not a station wagon? When it's based on a car platform and not a larger truck chassis, such as this 1969 GMC 'Suburban,' complete with Airstream RV. (Author's collection)

1950–1959: Flamboyant style with functionality

While some of the independent American automakers chose alternative solutions in order to provide station wagon qualities in sedan models, others

Ford's Edsel was considered a flop by many, particularly from a styling point of view, but the 116-inch (295cm) wheelbase, two- and four-door, six- and nine-passenger 1958 Roundup, Villager, and Bermuda V8-powered wagons initially sold well enough, achieving 63,110 units, although, by 1960, that figure had tumbled to a measly 2846 units. When introduced, many magazines of the day thought the styling "unique" and "distinctive." Motor Trend (10/57) also noted: "The Edsel performs fine, rides well, and handles good." (Author's collection)

With little or no domestic rivals in its size and price range, and much smaller foreign competition, early 1952 Rambler station wagons owned the 'Compact' market in North America at this time. Rambler wagon sales topped 24,000 units. (Author's collection)

competed head-on with the 'Big Three': Ford, GM, and Chrysler.

Leader amongst the independent American automakers was Nash; first with its Nash Rambler, and then as AMC with its eventual full Rambler line-up.

Yet, although throughout the 1950s Nash built large sedans with station wagon qualities, it was the smaller

Nash Rambler that created a new compact wagon market.

Nash was the first to offer a 'compact' car that provided style, comfort and typical American spaciousness at a lower price and overall smaller size, as well as providing better fuel economy. A total of 34,185 Nash Rambler station wagons were sold in 1951, and although that figure would not be matched again until 1959, production remained at around 20,000 wagons

Packard wasn't the only company that did not always use the term 'station wagon,' as a model description. Nash preferred to call its compact Rambler wagon an "All-Purpose sedan," though it was sometimes described in ads as "… two cars in one. A luxuriously appointed family sedan, it converts into a spacious station wagon – with a six-foot platform – at the drop of a hat." (Author's collection)

For its Golden Anniversary, in Canada Nash offered its 1952 Rambler Airflyte wagons in four versions: top-of-the-line Country Club; Custom; the Suburban, and the basic Deliveryman, all featuring Farina styling. A 'Greenbriar' version was also available in two-tone paint, sans faux woodgrain around the windows. The 82hp, L-head, 172.6cu in (2.8L), inline, six-cylinder engine was standard. American golfing great Sam Snead helped promote the wagons. (Author's collection)

Two Smart All-Purpose Sedans for Family or Business Use!

NASH RAMBLER "GREENBRIER"

This two-tone beauty distinguishes any company. The smart upholstery selections blend with the exterior color combinations. The rear seat lowers flush with the floor—as in the Custom Station Wagon model—to provide a load carrying platform over six feet long.

NASH RAMBLER "SUBURBAN"

America's most practical utility car . . . smart in appearance . . . economical to operate. Front seat accommodates three passengers. Rear seat lowers for additional load capacity. Available in wide choice of solid body colors.

For 1953, Rambler All-Purpose sedans were offered in luxury 'Greenbrier' trim, or in more basic guise such as the 'Suburban.' The optional hood ornament was designed by artist George Petty IV, famous for his 'Petty Girl' pin-ups, many of which graced the noses of US aircraft during WWII. (Author's collection)

a year for all Nash/Hudson/AMC/Rambler compact wagons. Even the Hudson Cross-Country sold well, with 13,024 finding buyers in 1955, the only year it was offered.

In the 1956 Coast-to-Coast Rambler Cross Country run, a randomly picked, stock Rambler '6' station wagon, fitted with automatic transmission and overdrive, left Disneyland Park in California, and traveled public roads and highways through desert, mountains and conurbations to New York City.

(continued p23)

AMC considered building a Metropolitan wagon, but, instead, its smallest station wagon was the compact 100-inch (250cm) wheelbase, two-door Pinin Farina Rambler Custom that first appeared on June 23, 1950. A four-door wagon joined the line-up for 1954. These compact Rambler wagons remained in production with only minor face-lifts until 1955, but were then dropped, only to be reintroduced in 1958. A two-door wagon version was included in 1959 and 1960. (Author's collection)

1954 saw an all-new Nash Rambler 'Cross Country' still described as a four-door, all-purpose sedan, as well as a "... spacious 15½ foot utility car with a smart new Travel-Rack for extra luggage atop the roof." Engine size had increased to 195.6cu in (3.2L), rated at 90hp. In 1956, Rambler would build its first four-door hardtop wagon, closely followed by its competitors, but this model, although stylish, had limited appeal to the more practical station wagon buyer. By the mid-1960s, few were offered. (Author's collection)

The Rambler Cross Country '6' proved it was king of station wagon economy by travelling coast-to-coast in 1956 on less than five tanks of gasoline. In fact, the above average fuel economy of its V8 engine was also proven in the 1956 Mobilgas Economy Run, when it topped all the other eight-cylinder competitors. (Author's collection)

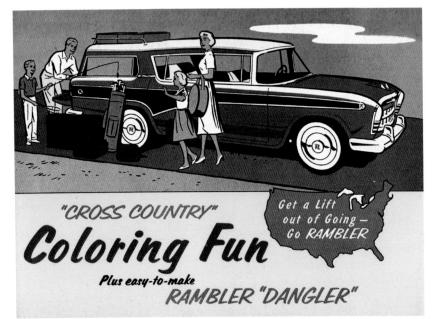

AMC advertising was aimed at the entire family – even American kids in 1957 with this free coloring book, available at showrooms across North America. In addition, there was a coast-to-coast puzzle maze, a Rambler sedan join-the-dots to see the 'Rambler's Double Safe Single Unit Construct,' and instructions for making "… a Rambler 'Dangler' mobile for your room!" (Author's collection)

SUPER CROSS COUNTRY "6"

This low-priced four-door station wagon is the most practical car on the boulevard . . . the finest "work and play" car for town or country. It's the most versatile car you can buy—a triple-duty beauty for work, for vacation, for family travel.

The new 1957 Rambler Super Cross Country '6' or V8 was typical of the stylish, yet highly practical wagons built by AMC in the 1950s. For 1957, the chic four-door Super Cross Country was offered in monotone, two- or three-tone paint schemes. With plenty of chrome, a trendy, shiny, rear half-roof rack labeled a 'Travel Rack,' full wheel discs, and wide whitewall tires, it had all the pizzazz of a Ford faux 'Woody' Country Squire, yet was competing in what Rambler termed "... the low price field." (Author's collection)

In advertising, storyboards and quotes from the company president were a popular way to get a message across, as can be seen in this 1957 Rambler Hudson and Nash magazine advertisement. Financial losses, though reduced, were still over 11 million dollars. AMC had turned the corner, though, and 1958 would see substantial profits. In fact, AMC was the only American car maker to make a profit in 1958, due to a mild economic recession. (Author's collection)

'58 Rambler —CROSS COUNTRY STATION WAGONS

CUSTOM CROSS COUNTRY 6 OR REBEL V-8
A white-tie-and-tails town sedan and a space-eating travel car!

SUPER CROSS COUNTRY 6 OR REBEL V-8 – Most practical station wagon on the market.

THE INSIDE STORY of the 1958 Rambler is a story of high fashion colors and fabrics. You'll admire the color-keyed interiors that represent the ultimate in good taste.

In 1958, the Hudson and Nash Rambler wagons grew fins, as had most American cars by this time. Yet, despite the existence of both Nash and Hudson nameplates in 1958, it was clear that the Rambler brand was the new future of American Motors for 1959. (Author's collection)

The new 1958 AMC model line-up (including station wagons) consisted of the Ambassador, Rebel 327cu in (5.4L), V8 models in Super and Custom versions, and two Cross Country 195.6cu in (3.2L), six-cylinder Super and Custom wagon models. Wagon sales soared to over 50,000 units to make AMC a profit of $26 million in 1958 after two years of losses. (Author's collection)

INTRODUCING THE DISTINGUISHED *Ambassador*
Station Wagon Family

CUSTOM 4-DOOR HARDTOP CROSS COUNTRY

SUPER 4-DOOR CROSS COUNTRY
Also available in Custom Series.

ROLL-DOWN REAR WINDOW—on all
station wagons disappears into tail-gate. Th
piece cargo door eliminates upper hinges . . .
more loading room.

As well as styling, a new feature of the 1958 Rambler was a one-piece, fold-down tailgate, thanks to the frameless rear window
that could be rolled down. By 1961, this idea had been adopted by the entire industry. Some of the option equipment on a
1958 Rambler wagon included: power brakes, steering, and windows; a push-button transistor radio; air conditioning; a padded
instrument panel; and push-button automatic transmission. (Author's collection)

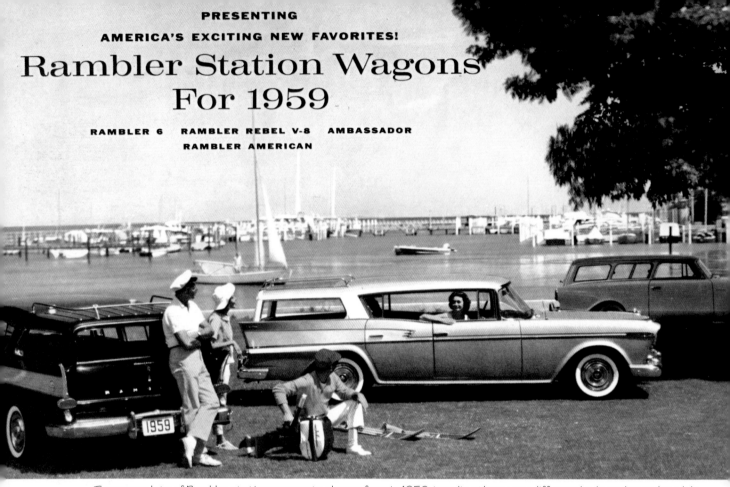

PRESENTING
AMERICA'S EXCITING NEW FAVORITES!
Rambler Station Wagons For 1959

RAMBLER 6   RAMBLER REBEL V-8   AMBASSADOR
RAMBLER AMERICAN

There were lots of Rambler station wagons to choose from in 1959, incuding three very different body styles and models. Standard power in the top-of-the-line Ambassador was the 270hp V8; in the Rambler, a choice of 215hp V8 in the Rebel or 127hp six in the Cross Country, and the American had a 90hp six-cylinder power unit. (Author's collection)

1960 was the last year for the old compact Rambler wagon that had first appeared in 1950, and later became known as the American model. The American nameplate would survive on subsequent compact models, including station wagons throughout the 1960s. (Author's collection)

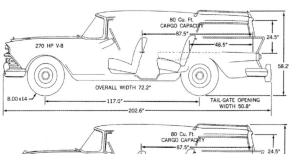

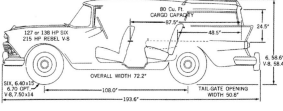

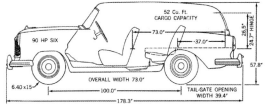

The 1959 Rambler station wagons were offered on three different wheelbases: 117-inch (297cm); 108-inch (274cm), or 100-inch (254cm), with an equally wide choice of powertrain. In 1959, AMC sold 374,240 cars, over 150,000 of which were station wagons. Despite the continuing recession, AMC was doing well with its smaller cars. (Author's collection)

As well as two drivers, a NASCAR official was onboard to ensure that every drop of gasoline was measured and the gas tank sealed after each fill-up. The 2961 mile (4765km) trip required only 77 imperial gallons (350L) of fuel for an average of 38.5mpg. Average speed over the distance was 40.3mph (65km/h).

Roll Down Rear Window on Cross Country Station Wagons disappears into tail-gate. The one-piece cargo door eliminates upper hinges ... gives more loading room.

Roof-Top Travel Rack gives extra carrying capacity ... adds to the distinctively smart appearance of Cross Country and American Super station wagons.

Twin Travel Beds and Airliner Reclining Seats—Cross Country exclusives—assure relaxing comfort. Seats adjust to 5 positions—make up into Twin Beds for restful all-night sleeping.

Kiddies' Play Pen is but one of the many uses to which the large cargo area can be put. Children can play the miles away in perfect safety .... even makes long trips a pleasure for all.

Sail Away To Pleasure in a Rambler Cross Country Station Wagon. Plenty of room for a boat plus all your baggage and gear in the big cargo space.

Air Coil Ride provides a level ride at all times regardless of road or load, increased stability when cornering. Available on all Cross Country Station Wagons.

The Rambler wagons were designed to satisfy all requirements, while offering great comfort and convenience, as can be seen in this special 'Rambler Station Wagons for 1959' brochure featuring all available models. (Author's collection)

In 1954 Studebaker introduced a two-door station wagon known as the 'Conestoga,' a name which stemmed from the company's historic pioneer roots. It came with plenty of options, including the Commander V8, subtle two-tone paintwork, wide whitewall tires, and full chrome wheel discs. Sales reached 10,651 units, with production remaining around that mark until the arrival of the compact Lark wagon in 1959. (Author's collection)

This new two-door wagon featured 64cu ft (1.8cu m) of cargo space, and was often referred to in advertisements as the "World's most beautiful station wagon!" and "… the most advanced station wagon of our times." Designed by the famed Raymond Loewy, the wagon borrowed the same styling themes as seen on his 1953 Starlight Coupe design, which had already won international praise and awards. (Author's collection)

However, as well as economy, the Rambler, powered by a 190hp V8 or the more economical 125hp straight six, was known for its 80cu ft (26cu m) of cargo space, and ability to haul a 4x8ft (1.2x2.4m) sheet of plywood.

The only real 'independent' competition to the economical AMC/Rambler wagons was offered by Studebaker, the great granddaddy of wagon builders, which built the Conestoga covered wagons that carried American pioneer families across the country in the 1800s, to open and settle the American 'wild west.'

Despite its great 'wagon' heritage, Studebaker was only a minor player in the station wagon market prior to WWII, and didn't produce any post-war station wagons until 1954, from which point it was responsible for numerous innovations in that area. Surprisingly, a four-door Studebaker wagon didn't appear until 1957; near the end of the line for its aging, 1953 body style.

Annual wagon sales amounted to only around 10,000 units until the all-new Lark compact wagon appeared in 1959, whereupon they more than doubled.

Packard re-entered the station wagon market in 1948, but, by 1950, had built its last wagon as an independent. Production of these wood-clad wagons was very minimal: in fact, the total number of Packard wagons – known as Standard Station Sedans – built from 1948 to the end of 1950 is an estimated 3864.

(continued p31)

At the 1956 Toronto Auto Show the largest crowd at the Studebaker-Packard display was gathered around the Packard Predictor show car, but note that the Studebaker Wagon appears to be drawing more attention than the company's sportier coupes. Despite this, wagon sales dipped below 10,000 units for the first time to just 6892 in 1956. (Author's collection)

1950s American cars were known for being well adorned when it came to chrome, and that included the family station wagon. This Studebaker was painted in original factory Air Force Blue Metallic and Daybreak Blue. (Courtesy Andrew Mort)

World's most beautiful station wagon!

White sidewall tires and chrome wheel discs optional in all models at extra cost.

In 1956 Studebaker's most powerful V8 was the 289cu in (4.7L) four-barrel, rated at 210hp, but as well as the standard six-cylinder, a smaller, 259cu in (4.2L) V8 was available to power your wagon. At this time, Studebaker had three assembly plants, including South Bend, Indiana, Los Angeles, California, and in Hamilton, Ontario, Canada. (Courtesy Andrew Mort)

Restyled in 1956, a bold, heavily chromed, front end still graced Studebaker sedans and wagons. The hood ornament was supposedly inspired by one created by LeBaron Coachworks. Designer Vince Gardner was responsible for overall styling. Surprisingly, despite consumer demand, Studebaker delivered only 69,593 cars that year. (Courtesy Andrew Mort)

This two-door, 1956 Studebaker Pinehurst wagon was powered by a four-barrel, 289cu in (4.7L) V8, and loaded with optional equipment such as power steering, air conditioning, a radio and clock, deluxe steering wheel, back-up lights, tinted glass, dual exhaust, full wheel discs, and whitewall tires. (Courtesy Andrew Mort)

Both interior and exterior styling in the 1950s was considered subdued, as this 1956 Studebaker Pinehurst wagon demonstrates. Not much in the way of restyling could be done with this tall, narrow body; particularly with Studebaker's limited funds. Still, various chrome trim, new colors, and a minor face-lift helped. Studebaker built only 6892 wagons in 1956. (Courtesy Andrew Mort)

Studebaker-Packard's line-up still included full-size Studebaker wagon models in 1957. This would soon change, as the company was already in the planning stage for its new, compact Lark. (Author's collection)

The 1957 Studebaker station wagon line-up consisted of three very different looking models. The two-door continued on, and two different four-door station wagon models were introduced. Rather than enjoying a substantial increase in sales, the two-door dropped almost 2000 units to just 5062 wagons. The four-door fared only marginally better, production reaching 5142 units. (Author's collection)

The old, mid-sized models were gone in 1959, as all eyes were on the latest compact from Studebaker. The all-new 1959 Studebaker Lark was promoted not only for its fun, versatility and 'marathon mileage,' but also its "... fashion-approved-by-Harper's Bazaar ..." interior styling. Now the only station wagon offered, it broke sales records, accounting for 25,474 units of the 126,156 cars built by Studebaker that year. (Author's collection)

29

Versatility was the mainstay of the Lark station wagon, with its optional eight-passenger or 93cu ft (2.6cu m) carrying capacity. It was available as a two-door only, though could seat eight, thanks to a rear-facing, hideaway benchseat. The wagon's turning diameter was impressive at just 39 feet (12m). (Author's collection)

Opposite: The 1958 Packard wagon featured the unique and rather unusual front end styling of the sporty Packard Hawk, four-door sedan and hardtop. The rear end featured dual fins on each fender; only fitting, given its fish-like front end. These Packards were powered by the company's 289cu in (4.7L) V8 rated at 225hp, had an overall length of 206.2 inches (524cm), and a 116.5-inch (296cm) wheelbase. (Author's collection)

Ad copy for the 1957 Packard Clipper Country Sedan models noted: "A new age of functional elegance arrives!" Despite low production numbers, the 1957 and 1958 Packard station wagons featured very different styling. The 1957 Packard Clipper Country Sedan (Packard's name for its station wagon) was very Studebaker-like in appearance. (Author's collection)

From the Home of the Golden Hawks...

The Packard Station Wagon

Over the years, there were few cosmetic changes; in the last year, essentially just trim and script were modified.

This figure seems huge in comparison with the number of later Studebaker-Packard station wagons to bear this once proud nameplate. In 1957, Studebaker-Packard produced a mere 869 Clipper Country Sedan station wagons, and in its final year as a brand only, 159 Packard station wagons were built.

Over at Willys, despite re-entering the car market in 1952, the only station wagon was still the Jeep-based version first introduced in 1946, and a 4x4 version in 1949. It remained in production – continually updated

– until 1965. Although never a high volume seller, sales surpassed 32,000 wagons in 1950.

The three major American automakers were quick to enter the rapidly expanding, highly competitive station wagon market in the 1950s, and continually offered new and exciting designs with more and more features. Often flamboyant color schemes and space age style provided an edge, but it was price, utility, reliability, and service that played decisive roles. Ford, Mercury, Chevrolet, Buick, Pontiac, Oldsmobile, Chrysler, Dodge, DeSoto and Plymouth parts and service were far more readily available, and the 'Big Three' had the financial strength to cut costs and therefore prices.

The 1955 Ford had lots of style, as can be seen in this two-tone Country Sedan. Ford sold 106,089 of its best selling four-door Country Sedan six-passenger ($2156US) and eight-passenger ($2287US) wagons that year, in comparison to the two-door Mainline Ranch wagon (40,493), the Custom Line (43,671), and the top-of-the-line Country Squire (19,011). Sales had leapt annually since a record 1950 level of 29,017 wagons. An eight-passenger Country Squire cost a hefty $2392US, the most expensive Ford model other than the new two-seater Thunderbird. Ford wagons had virtually the exact same chassis as the Ford car line-up, other than heavy duty shocks and heftier springs. (Author's collection)

For 1957 the Ford line was completely restyled, and the more angular, finned wagons in two- and four-door versions topped over 300,000 units. The Ranch Wagon was the base model. The wagons were 213.5 inches (542cm) in overall length, virtually 16 inches (41cm) longer than the 1956 models. (Author's collection)

Ford continued to dominate the station wagon market into the 1950s with its range of Ranch Wagons, Country Squires and Country Sedans in two-door and four-door, six- and eight-passenger versions. Ford had built the first mass-produced station wagons which coincided with the introduction of the Model A in 1928. Founder Henry Ford was a keen outdoors man, and enthusiastic camper who went on outings regularly with friends, Harry Firestone, Thomas Edison, and naturalist John Burroughs, in Model Ts. Henry Ford's inbred interest and enthusiasm was clearly evident in

Opposite: By 1959, the Ford full-size station wagon was in its last year of the three year cycle. A new rear and front end treatment, paint combinations and colors and trim helped set it apart from its predecessors. With a choice of six different wagons came the choice of two Thunderbird V8 engines, rated at 225hp or 303hp, or the more economical 145hp six-cylinder. There were also three transmissions available – a two-speed or three-speed automatic, or a three-speed manual with column shift. (Author's collection)

Ford wagon sales numbered over 268,000 units in 1959 with the two-door Ranch wagon accounting for less than 10 per cent of that at 27,136 in sales. This was the least expensive wagon powered by Ford's Mileage Maker six-cylinder engine. As pointed-out in the Ford brochure "… You'll enjoy the thriftiest 'wagon transportation' since the ox-drawn Prairie Schooner! Example: you change your oil only every 4000 miles instead of the 1000 often recommended." (Author's collection)

The up-market Ford Mercury line had two of its own four-door station wagons based on the Ford. Styling, materials and trim differed on the dressier Mercury models. The highest priced Mercury Monterey station wagon had all the features of the Country Squire, and more. Options included power steering and brakes, four-way seats, and power lubrication. By pressing a button on the dash, it was possible to lubricate the entire chassis, steering, and suspension system. A Custom, and other lower-priced Mercury models were offered in 1955. (Author's collection)

the company's continued vigorous pursuit of the wagon market.

Ford went so far as to publish – via Simon & Schuster – hardcover books of over 250 pages, entitled

Ford Treasury of Station Wagon Living Volume #1 1957; *Ford Treasury of Station Wagon Living Volume #2* 1958, and *The Ford Guide to Outdoor Living On Wheels* (circa 1959). These books – about enjoying station wagons – were written by Ford employees and its customers. Filled with creative, do-it-yourself ideas, new products and accessories, camping tips, and ways of using your Ford station wagon to its fullest potential, the books helped increase sales by taking advantage of the interest in outdoor living.

Ford also built the 'Push-button Camper of the Future' concept vehicle in 1958, which featured a spring-loaded, pop-up tent on the roof of a Country Squire; a push-button rear tailgate awning, and a tent cover that turned into a small boat. Inside, a kitchen included a sink, refrigerator, and hidden compartment for an outboard boat motor!

While sales and interest in station wagons had increased since WWII, it wasn't until after the Korean War that the market fully blossomed. The increase in leisure time, improved production methods, booming camping and recreational equipment market, highway expansion, better roads, more and more state, provincial and national parks, all perpetuated the interest of North Americans in owning a station wagon.

Major innovations, such as folding rear seats and the roll-down window in the rear tailgate (introduced

The Mercury Monterey could be ordered with three different colors for the cloth (Chromatex) and vinyl interior in 1955 – red, blue or green. Other interior niceties included coat hooks, armrests, interior courtesy lights, a cigarette lighter, and a handy robe cord. With the centre seat folded you had 32.6cu ft. (0.9cu m) of space and with the tailgate dropped another 6.7cu ft (0.2cu m). A total of 11,968 Monterey wagons were delivered in 1955. (Author's collection)

STYLELINE DE LUXE STATION WAGON

Chevrolet began the decade already committed to all-steel versions. By 1951, it was promoting the safety of all-steel, unibody construction in its station wagon with the "… smartness and distinction of a wood-grain finish." With four doors and three rows of seats, it allowed easy access, but that third seat had to be physically removed in order to increase load capacity. (Author's collection)

Lagging well behind traditional industry leader Ford, in wagon sales, apart from its conventional station wagon, Chevrolet unveiled the Nomad. The two-door Nomad was, "… an experimental model, combining the sleek styling of a sports car with the versatility and utility of a Station Wagon." It was introduced at the 1954 General Motors Motorama, designed to attract greater attention and increase wagon sales. As a result of the response there, the Nomad went into production in mid-1955, and Chevrolet became the first American manufacturer to build the soon-to-be-popular hardtop wagon. (Author's collection)

The Chevrolet nomad

Despite its styling flair, 1955 Nomad sales were disappointing at just 6103 wagons. The 115-inch (292cm) six-seater wagon was available with a choice of six- or eight-cylinder engine, and featured the up-market Bel Air interior trim at a base price of $2571US. In comparison, the standard two-door wagon sold for $2079US, which was a substantial difference in price in 1955. Pontiac offered an equivalent 'Safari' version, but by 1958 it and the unique-bodied Nomad had disappeared. (Author's collection)

GM's Pontiac Division's station wagons shared the same bodyshell as the popular Chevrolet model, but lacked the styling pizzazz of its sibling throughout the 1950s, and always played second fiddle to Chevrolet. This was set to change soon with the new 'Wide Track Pontiacs' and performance models of the 1960s. Pictured is a 1957 Canadian Super Chief. In the fifties, slightly up-market Pontiac lagged well behind Chevrolet with total station wagon sales of all models reaching a mere 39,919 units by 1959. (Courtesy Howard Furtak)

by Chrysler in 1950), also had a major impact on sales. Previously, rear seats required unbolting and removal, while the lift-up tailgate was restrictive, cumbersome, and heavy.

Ford station wagon sales had grown from 16,960 'Woodies' in 1946 to 31,412 steel-bodied wagons in 1949. In retrospect that's a minor increase, as sales rocketed to 141,582 wagons in 1954, and 269,338 units in 1959, together with 74,310 two- and four-door compact Ford Falcon station wagons, and 44,891 Edsel wagons.

Ford's Mercury division also offered a wagon, though sales were comparatively low: just 11,656 units in 1954. Yet, by 1959, a total of 173,541 full-size Mercury and compact Comet station wagons were delivered to proud owners.

In comparison, longtime rival Chevrolet built just 810 'Woody' wagons in 1946, which increased to only 6006 units by 1949. In 1954, sales of Chevrolet's

(continued p42)

With its new look in 1954, Buick introduced a wagon line-up which included four-door Century and Special models. Buick noted in its brochure, "Front-Page News In More Ways Than One Is The All-Steel Buick Estate – for this famed Buick body style now comes … in a new, lower price range – and with the sheer brilliance of Century performance." The Special six-passenger 'Estate Wagon' (pictured) was built on a 122-inch (310cm) wheelbase fitted with a 264cu in (4.3L) 150hp V8, while the up-market Century was powered by a 322cu in (5.3L) 200hp V8. (Author's collection)

Despite Buick's luxury wagon image of the past, both 1954 models were promoted as budget-priced. This was due more to the fact that the 'Woody' wagon had cost from $3254US to $3430US in 1953, of which Buick sold 5148 wagons. The new 1954 Special and Century (pictured) all-steel station wagons were listed at $3163US and $3470US, yet just 3212 found willing customers. Buick had sold just 2900 'woodies' in 1950 and was not a major player in the station wagon market with sales reaching only 13,517 units in 1959. (Author's collection)

This list price $3265US, 1958, Buick Riviera, 4-door Estate was the mid-range model in 1958 and accounted for 3420 sales, whereas the top-of-the-line $3383US Century wagon attracted 4456 buyers. Still, Buick wagon sales were minimal in comparison to the rest of the American car industry. (Author's collection)

1958 Oldsmobile Super 88 Fiesta was the only model available in this series, but shared the same basic body with its sister, Dynamic 88. Oldsmobile's re-entry into the station wagon market in 1957, with its hardtop-like styling, was the most expensive wagon in the line-up at $3623US. Note the Hollywood film setting with comedian Jerry Lewis of Martin and Lewis fame waiting for his ride. In 1950, in its last year of station wagon production, Oldsmobile sold 1750 'Woody' wagons. In 1959 station wagon sales had only increased to 18,313 units. (Courtesy Thomas McPherson)

Dashing!

Here is space with the sweetest lines on wheels. Whatever your mode of living, the versatile Fiesta will meet your needs!

Fiesta's cargo space is up 13%
lost year, and there's more
room and hip room for pas-
gers as well. Second seat fea-
s simplified release mecha-
, Electric window lift for new
actable rear window and ⅓-⅔
ded second seat are available.

dynamic 88 fiesta

Oldsmobile also offered station wagons throughout the decade for its loyal customers. Like Buick, Olds sales rose slowly but steadily. In 1959, the two all-new styled Oldsmobile station wagons included the pricey $3365US Fiesta model in the Dynamic 88 model range. Special options included an electric rear tailgate window, and a one-third/two-third split rear folding bench seat. (Author's collection)

Pricier than the Dynamic 88 Fiesta wagon, the more powerful 315hp V8 Super 88 Fiesta wagon was priced at $3669US, and found 7015 buyers in 1959. The jet-inspired styling was referred to as the 'Linear look.' The Dynamic and Super models featured a 9-inch (23cm) wider and 10-inch (25cm) longer frame. Cargo space increased by 13 per cent over 1958 models. This model set a new wagon production record for Oldsmobile in 1959 by achieving sales of 11,298 units. (Author's collection)

Chrysler offered station wagons in all four of its car lines. Plymouth had offered a 'Woody' station wagon in its line-up since 1938, and resumed production following WWII. In 1949, Plymouth offered its first all-steel as well as 'Woody' wagon, which sold in minimal numbers until 1950. All 1951 'Suburban' wagons were steel. This dressier Plymouth Cranbrook Savoy (Suburban) found 12,089 enthusiastic owners in 1953. (Author's collection)

Chrysler sold its vehicles through Dodge-DeSoto and Chrysler-Plymouth dealers. Those customers wanting to move up-market could continue with the same dealer by moving to a DeSoto or a Chrysler. Although fancier than a Dodge, the DeSoto was available with either the 116hp Powermaster Six or 170hp FireDome V8. The 1954 DeSoto models featured the 'Forward Look' – a styling term Chrysler would re-use often over the next five decades. (Author's collection)

Like some others, in 1954 Chrysler was still building its all-steel station wagon with a wooden floor. This tradition would soon disappear, too. This restored 1954 Chrysler New Yorker wagon is fitted with a 331cu (5.4L) in Hemi V8, and features an automatic transmission, power steering and brakes, and electric windows. (Courtesy Wes Ball)

3 WIDE-VIEW OBSERVATION SEAT! Easy to enter. Folds flush in floor when not in use. A Plymouth low-price 3 exclusive. You have to lift out 3rd seat of "other two."

4 REAR WINDOW DISAPPEARS! Another Plymouth exclusive in its field! Window rolls into lower section. No clumsy overhanging tailgate for Plymouth owners.

5 AND IT RIDES WITH BIG CAR LUXURY! Floating Tors Aire Ride—Plymouth's top-luxury ride at no extra c No sway or lurch on turns... no nose-dive on sto

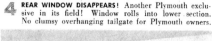

Plymouth was Chrysler's volume station wagon, and in 1958, with its famous 'fin' models, the Division sold over 115,000 of them. These buyers had discovered the five big reasons why their next station wagon should be a Plymouth, including the soon-to-be-adopted, industry-wide rear facing seat (a Chrysler innovation introduced in 1957), which folded neatly into the floor, was easier to access, and provided far more footroom. (Author's collection)

Handyman and Townsman wagons had risen to 56,735 units, and by 1959, Chevrolet had closed the gap considerably with sales of 209,383 station wagons.

Meanwhile, over at Chrysler, De Soto, Dodge and Plymouth, it was the Plymouth line of wagons that were the big sellers at 2057 sales in 1950, which increased to 120,802 by 1959. Dodge Division accounted for around another 23,500 station wagons in '59.

The 1959, 122-inch (310cm) wheelbase Plymouth station wagon had its own brochure to highlight all of its features. With the tailgate down and all seats folded, the wagon provided 120 inches (305cm) or 100cu ft (2.8cu m) of storage space. Overall length with tailgate closed was 214 inches (544cm). (Author's collection)

1960-1969: More of everything

In 1951, American station wagon sales totaled 174,500 – 3.3 per cent of the car market in the United States; by 1960, this figure had leapt to 932,000 units, or 15.4 per cent of the American car market.

The Checker Superba was announced in 1959, but sold as a 1960 model. The Superba had a floor length of 109 inches (277cm) from the back of the front seat at floor level to the end of the lowered tailgate, and a floor length of 69.25 inches (176cm) from the back of the second seat to the end of the lowered tailgate. When the tailgate was closed and the front seat pushed forward as far as possible, the amount of floor space was a remarkable 96 inches (244cm). Maximum width was 48.5 inches (123cm), and there were no intruding rear wheelarches. This full-size wagon would also be offered in stretch form as well, to cater for the airport limousine business. (1962 Marathon pictured.)
(Author's collection)

In 1962, standard equipment on the Checker station wagons included a heater, defroster, padded instrument panel, and 6.70x15, 4-ply tires. Everything else was optional, including any power-assist items, as well as basics such as back-up lights, an outside rear mirror, and an oil filter. Yet, by this time, the option list had grown considerably, and included items such as power windows, seat belts, tinted glass, air conditioning – and even an auxiliary under-seat heater at extra cost. In addition, a power rear seat was available for the station wagon, as was a full luggage rack. Although the Checker station wagon version was perhaps not the most stylish, it made up for that in size and exclusivity.
(Author's collection)

One of the largest station wagon models of the 1960s was the Checker Superba. Checker Motors Corporation of Kalamazoo, Michigan, was established by Morris Markin in 1923, and built taxi cabs. In 1933, it became part of E L Cord's conglomerate, which also produced Auburn, Cord, and Duesenberg cars. In 1936,

Throughout the 1960s the American Station wagon was promoted as the symbol of family holidays and the great outdoors, as demonstrated by this 1961 brochure. Chevrolet also promoted itself with the line "See the USA in your Chevrolet!" Pictured is the nine-passenger Nomad. (Author's collection)

Cord was in financial difficulties, and sold his holdings in Checker to Markin. (Both were later investigated by the US government for stock manipulation.)

Meanwhile, production continued and, following WWII, in 1947 a redesigned version of Checker's popular, spacious taxicab appeared with an announcement that, in 1948, a Checker could be ordered as a private 'pleasure' car.

In 1954, assembly was halted in preparation for an all-new Checker, but full production didn't resume until 1956. A mild redesign occurred in 1958, and new passenger car models were announced. By 1960, a station wagon version was introduced which led to a very unique 'stretch' limousine version of the wagon, known as the Aerobus, in both six- and eight-door styles. Options on the rather basic Checker included a more powerful 140hp, Continental, six-cylinder engine.

In 1962, the 40th anniversary of the 120-inch (305cm) wheelbase Checker was celebrated by the announcement of over 200 amendments, with 93 mechanical improvements and minor styling and interior upgrades. Checkers were still powered by a 141hp ohv or 80hp L-Head 226cu in (3.7L) six-cylinder Continental engine. Despite an increase in horsepower, this wasn't a lot of capability with which to move the 3780lb (1715kg) station wagon.

Available in two trim levels, the more luxurious four-door Checker Marathon station wagon featured added trim outside and all the niceties inside, and was advertised as 'The Town and Country Car.' The more functional, basic Superba station wagon was described as a 'Big Car Ride with Small Car Economy.' The Superba name was dropped at the end of 1964, as was the six-cylinder Continental engine, which was replaced by a 250cu in (4.0L) Chevrolet six-cylinder unit. Later that year, Checker announced its models could now be ordered with a Chevrolet 283cu in (4.6L), later followed in 1965 by the introduction of the optional Chevrolet 327cu in (5.4L) V8. Some Checkers in 1963-64 were powered by Chrysler engines.

Outwardly, few changes occurred throughout production of the Checker station wagon, but Checker was one of the first American automobiles to be offered with a diesel engine in 1968. Attempts were made to build niche custom models and limos, but, after a turbulent 1970s, the last Checker left the factory on July 12, 1982.

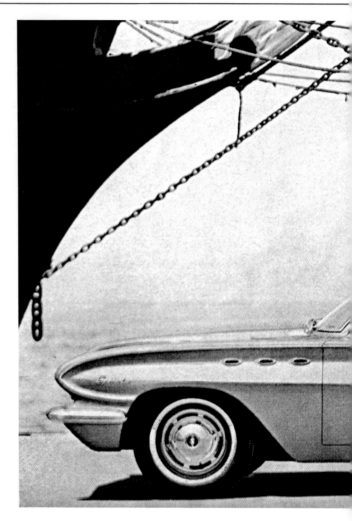

Things may have been very different had its new owner, former GM president Ed Cole, not died in a plane crash in May 1977, amidst the planning of an all-new Checker, which was subsequently aborted.

Buick also introduced a smaller compact line in 1961, based on Corvair tooling. The Buick Special was available as a full range of models, including a 112-inch (284cm) wheelbase, two-seat and three-seat station wagon powered by a lightweight aluminum V8. Styling was similar to the larger Buick models. Despite the fact that a V6 version was also offered in 1962, wagon sales rose only marginally from 18,628 in 1961 to just 20,576 in 1962. (Author's collection)

SUPER 88 FIESTA (available in 2 and 3-seat models)

The 1960 123-inch (312cm) wheelbase Oldsmobile Super 88 Fiesta was available as a two-seat or three-seat wagon, and had 88cu ft (2.5cu m) of cargo space with the second and third row seats folded. All Super 88 models were powered by the more potent 315hp V8. That year, 3765 two-seat Super 88 Fiesta wagons were sold, as well as 3475 three-seat versions. (Author's collection)

Like the other GM divisions, Oldsmobile introduced its own version of a smaller, compact, four-door wagon in 1961. F-85 four-door wagon sales in both Standard and DeLuxe, two-seat and three-seat forms were just under 18,000 units. The DeLuxe models cost about $300US more than the Standard at $2816US, and included a deluxe steering wheel and padded dash, front and rear carpeting, and other minor trim features. Standard power was the 155hp 'Rockette' V8. (Author's collection)

This fully rebuilt 1962 Oldsmobile Fiesta wagon was converted to a sporty 'Starfire' for a mild custom-look by changing all its outside trim. Although very stylish, it was never a production model. (Courtesy Andrew Mort)

1962 Oldsmobile Fiesta interiors were luxurious and well appointed. The ($3460US) two-seat Fiesta wagon outsold the three-seat version ($3568US), 8527 to 6417 units, despite the fact that price differential was just over $100US. Although minimal exterior changes were made, the V8 engines were improved, as was the HydraMatic transmission. (Courtesy Andrew Mort)

OLDSMOBILE STATION WAGONS *WHERE THE ACTION IS!*

Introducing the all new VISTA-CRUISER

The all-new 1964 Oldsmobile Vista Cruiser, with its raised roofline and added glass, provided a sense of openness, as well as extra sunlight and additional headroom for those passengers in the second and third row seating. Unveiled at that year's Chicago Auto Show, the styling cues were to be shared by Buick, as well as the Olds F85 and Cutlass wagons for a time. The Oldsmobile Vista Cruiser went on to become an industry leader, yet its unique profile was never copied. (Courtesy Thomas McPherson)

1961 saw the introduction of the Safari Wagon as a model in the new Pontiac Tempest line-up in Standard and DeLuxe versions. The Standard wagon was powered by a four-cylinder engine, created by slicing in half a 389cu in (6.4L) V8. The engine became known as the 'Iron Duke,' although referred to by Pontiac in 1961 as the 'Indy Four.' (Author's collection)

General Motors, with its many divisions, two distinct dealership brands, and customer loyalty, offered most of its wagons with the same body, but different styling features and engine configurations.

Buick and Oldsmobile buyers were looking for different things in their wagons. Over the decade, Oldsmobile emerged as the more expensive, high performance division, but when the 'muscle car era' heated-up, the waters became muddied. Buick began offering more performance as well as luxury, and Oldsmobile, with its hot 442 'muscle car,' offered the same performance in a wagon version.

As well as the Falcon, Ford also marketed its traditional full-size, two- and four-door wagons, including the nine- and six-passenger Country Sedans, the Tudor and Fordor Ranch Wagon, and the Galaxie Country Squire. The 1960 Ford Galaxie Country Squire was the top-of-the-line Ford wagon, immediately identifiable by its imitation plastic and paper wood-grain sides. Ford sold 22,237 of these luxury wagons that year. (Author's collection)

9-passenger Country Sedan

Fordor Ranch Wagon

6-passenger Country Sedan

Tudor Ranch Wagon

9-passenger Country Squire

Opposite: During the 1950s and sixties, the Canadian Pontiacs were different from the American models in terms of available powerplants, name plates, trim, and styling cues. This is a full-size, V8-powered Canadian 1963 Pontiac Parisienne Safari Wagon, the equivalent of the American Catalina model. In Canada, these large wagons were also available as a mid-range Laurentian or base Strato Chief. (Author's collection)

Meanwhile, Pontiac – which had a 'granny car' image in 1959 – was to become the 'wide track Pontiac,' and a performance division under the guidance of Bunkie Knudsen, Pete Estes, and John DeLorean. The focus was on the sportier Grand Prix, Tempest, GTO, and later Firebird models, rather than station wagons.

Ford maintained its domination of the wagon market in the 1960s by adding both compact and

Added to the 1960 line-up was the new, compact Ford Falcon, available in a full range of body styles, including a two-door and four-door wagon. Initially a mild sales success with 27,552 units in two-door guise and 46,758 in four-door wagons, these figures would soar in 1961 to over 129,000; the four-door wagon accounting for 87,933 units, and a sales leader in the compact wagon class. (Author's collection)

intermediate-sized wagons to its line-up. The compact Falcon was introduced in 1960, followed by the Fairlane wagon in 1963. Both lines would prove very popular over the decade, as was Ford's traditional, full-size wagon.

During this period competition was fierce, and major styling changes occurred on a three-year cycle, and sometimes after just two years. Buyers expected annual model face-lifts (minor styling changes to the

(continued p59)

Try this one for size!

Ford's American full-size wagons weren't just limited to North America, as seen in this September 23, 1960 *Autocar* advertisement. Ford of Canada was ready to export to Britain a right-hand-drive Galaxie Country Sedan with room for nine, and 41sq ft (3.8sq m) of floor area. (Author's collection)

This top trim 1966 Ford Country Squire was one of 41,953 nine-passenger Country Squire wagons sold that year, plus 27,645 six-passenger versions. Total full-size Ford wagon production reached 178,751 units. This Country Squire was equipped with the optional 275hp, 390cu in (6.4L) V8 engine, automatic transmission, power steering and brakes, factory air conditioning, tinted glass with shaded windshield, power windows (including rear tailgate window), power seats, remote control outside and day/night inside rear view mirrors, original AM radio, and more. (Courtesy *The Stable*)

The innovative dual tailgate gave Ford a sizeable edge in the station wagon market in 1966, and was hailed as one of the decade's leading engineering advances, as loading and unloading was much easier. It was dubbed the 'New Magic Doorgate' and was available on all Ford station wagons. Another feature was the facing third row seating. (Author's collection)

Now it's a door . . . for easier entry or close-up loading. New Magic Doorgate is shown on the '66 Ford Country Squire. Notice the dual-facing rear seats in this model.

Now it's a tailgate! Used as a conventional tailgate, the Magic Doorgate extends the loadspace for long cargo, can also serve as a platform or picnic table.

Opposite: Ford's compact Falcon had been restyled in 1964, and then again in 1966 with a longer hood; it boasted great head and shoulder room, and 11 per cent more cargo space. It was one of nine different Ford station wagons available in three different station wagon sizes. The compact Falcon, intermediate Fairlane, and full-size Country models shared a family resemblance. (Author's collection)

Corvair was really Chevrolet's answer to the Volkswagen, and the maker even went so far as to adopt the rear-engine, air-cooled engine concept. Larger, with 10cu ft (2.8cu m) as well as 58cu ft (1.6cu m) of rear-loading space, it also offered four-door, six-passenger convenience, and came in a dozen colors, plus seven two-tone combinations for 1961. Sales were substantial in 1961 at 26,042 wagons, but collapsed in 1962 to around 6000 units, due to the introduction of the compact Chevy II. (Author's collection)

Opposite: Ford's Fairlane models were new for '66. These cars followed the then current trend of longer, lower, and wider. The 1966 intermediate-sized six- and eight-passenger Ford Fairlane station wagons came in three levels of trim, and in both six-cylinder and V8 forms, including a brand-new Squire, 11,558 examples of which were sold. A total of 12,379 Ranch wagons found buyers, as did 19,826 Custom versions. Cargo space measured out at 93.4cu ft (2.6cu m). (Author's collection)

When the Corvair was restyled in 1965, a wagon wasn't offered, though the equally compact, better-selling, more conventional, boxy, six-passenger Chevy II wagon (first seen in 1962) *was* available with a choice of different six- and eight-cylinder engines, including a 350hp, 327cu in (5.4L) V8. Although it had ample height, width and length were criticized: with the second seat folded and tailgate shut, the length was a very acceptable 86 inches (218cm), but tailgate width was only 47 inches (119cm), which restricted loads. When restyled in 1968, the Chevy II wagon was dropped. (Author's collection)

STATION WAGON IN ARBOR GREEN   STATION WAGON IN HONDURAS MA

NOMAD 4-DOOR 9-PASSENGER STATION WAGON

For 1961, Chevy styling was once again extensively re-modelled for an all-new look, and the wagons were offered as six different models: three six-passenger and three nine-passenger. The full-size Chevrolets were shorter and taller by 2 inches (5cm), in response to criticism regarding headroom. All the wagons featured a new, concealed compartment under the rear platform. The rear tailgate was over 9 inches (22.5cm) wider and slightly taller. Maximum cargo space was a generous 97.5cu ft (2.7cu m). (Author's collection)

Extensive restyling made the '63 full-size Chevy appear all-new, and a total of 198,00 full-size wagons were produced in 1963. This pristine, nine-passenger, top-of-the-line Chevrolet Impala wagon appears completely original, except for its 1968 Corvette wheels. It was built in Los Angeles, California, and features factory A/C, automatic transmission, luggage rack, factory dual exhaust, air-lift rear shocks, power brakes, push-button radio with rear speaker, a soft-ray tinted windshield, and a 250hp, 327cu in (5.4L) V8. (Courtesy Peter Preuss)

Many North Americans feel the full-size 1966 Chevy was the best American car ever made, and Chevrolet offered fourteen different station wagon models that year. The flagship wagon was the full-size, four-door wagon Impala complete with wood-grain panels. Optional was a 427cu in (7.0L) 425hp Turbo-Jet V8. (Author's collection)

The intermediate Chevelle was a very popular model, and the 'muscle car' of choice in the Chevrolet line, but the smaller, lighter Chevy II wagon also had a big V8, and lots of horsepower in the wagon range. The Chevelle four-door wagon was available as a well-dressed Malibu with lots of options, or as a very basic, functional 300 DeLuxe. (Author's collection)

Chrysler continued to offer the corporation's flagship station wagon, although sharing the same basic bodyshell with its sibling divisions. In 1962, the Chrysler Newport wagon was offered as two-seat and three-seat versions, but sales were a mere 3271 and 2363 respectively. In the highest trim level, the New Yorker wagons accounted for even fewer at just 728 and 793 in two- and three-seat forms. (Author's collection)

grille, taillights, and trim), and these were done every year until the next all-new model appeared.

1966 marked a design innovation from Ford that would soon be adopted by the entire industry. Ford's dual-action tailgate opened as a door, or folded like a conventional tailgate, which provided owners with easier loading, unpacking, egress and ingress.

Ford's highly popular Country Squire continued to be a best-seller throughout the decade and into the 1970s. The wood-look was still a popular choice for wagon buyers, and was offered by every American manufacturer.

Ford's greatest rival in wagon sales was Chevrolet. As the decade began in 1961, rear-engine, compact Corvair wagon sales were substantial, but soon collapsed with the introduction of the more conventional front engine, rear-wheel-drive, compact Chevy II in 1962. Although Chevy just lagged behind Ford in wagon sales – with a total of 212,729 in 1960 – the gap would grow as total Chevrolet full-size and intermediate wagon sales in 1968 reached around 221,100 units only.

In 1960, Ford sold 171,824 full-size station wagons, and in 1969 built 238,523. **Ford station wagons accounted for a total of 295,517 sales in all three of**

This 1966 Chrysler Town and Country wagon is an unrestored Canadian survivor, still wearing most of its original two-tone paint, as ordered by a Regina Saskatchewan dealer as a demonstrator. Note that the lower side moldings are white rather than the standard wood-grain appliqué. Powerful V8s were available even for the station wagons during the muscle car era, and this wagon was fitted with the optional 365hp, 440cu in (7.2L) 'TNT' V8 engine. (The TNT designation stood for twin snorkel air intake and dual exhaust, and was an extra cost option over the standard 440cu in (7.2L).)
(Courtesy Russ Wooldridge)

This 1966 Chrysler even provided third row, rearward-facing passengers with the luxury of air conditioning. Other luxury options include 'Autopilot' cruise control, front and rear A/C with tinted glass, reclining bucket seats, a 'Twilight Safety Sentinel Headlight System' (a programmable photocell which turned on headlights when ambient light was dim, as well as remaining on for up to 90 seconds when the ignition was switched off), an AM Search Tuner Radio which automatically sought-out the next station with the press of a floor switch), four-way flashers, a clock, two-tone paint, disc brakes, power windows, dual air conditioning, and a full roof rack. With both seats folded, an 8 foot (2.4m) loading floor was made available. Chrysler wagon sales were increasing slowly and, by 1966, reached 9035 two-seat versions and 8567 three-seat luxury wagons.
(Courtesy Russ Wooldridge)

its model lines in 1969, compared with 246,134 from its two models in 1960. (These figures do not include the equivalent Mercury compact Comet, and full-size Commuter and Colony Park station wagons.) The higher priced, slightly up-market Mercury station wagon totals were 138,691 in 1960 – its last year with unique styling. The rest of the decade Mercury shared the Ford-based bodies, and by 1969 sales were just 46,057 units.

Still, although luxury wagons were never huge volume sellers, even Chrysler, the third-largest American car manufacturer, continued to offer top-of-the line

wagons throughout the decade, and was the last to offer a hardtop wagon in 1964.

For example, in 1966, Chrysler's Town and Country station wagons in either nine- or six-passenger guise were available with a wide choice of V8 power. You could order your Town and Country with a standard 325hp,

Seven different Plymouth wagons were available in 1960 as two- or four-door, six- or nine-passenger models in a Custom and DeLuxe series, as well as this Sport Suburban with its two-tone paint, full wheel discs, and wide, whitewall tires. (Author's collection)

Inserted by Chrysler Corporation of Canada, Limite

VALIANT
THE VALUEST VALUE EVE!

V-100 FOUR-DOOR STATION WAGON

V-200 FOUR-DOOR SEDAN

Completely restyled in 1963, the Plymouth Valiant turned out to be a real winner in the compact car market. The standard engine was Chrysler's 101hp, or optional 145hp slant six, which proved bulletproof, as well as provided excellent fuel mileage. Three trim levels were offered: the V-100, V-200, and Signet 200. (Author's collection)

383cu in (6.3L) V8, or move up three more levels to a 365hp, 440cu in (7.2L) V8 with an Torqueflite automatic transmission. Standard equipment included power-operated steering/**brakes**/rear tailgate glass, plus fender-mounted front turn signal indicators, back-up lights, a 3-speed automatic transmission, and a carpeted luggage area. Prices of the nine-passenger wagons started at $6003US. Yet, it was Plymouth, more so than Dodge, which was the volume station wagon brand for the Chrysler Corporation.

Fury was the high end, 121-inch (307cm) wheelbase Plymouth line in 1966. You could order a Fury I, II or III wagon, with the Fury III being the best. All could be had as a six- or nine-passenger wagon. The six-seat wagon provided a 10.3cu ft (0.29cu m) luggage compartment with a latching cover. The third seat of the nine-passenger model faced rearward. A six-cylinder, or choice of three higher performance V8 engines were available. (Author's collection)

In 1960, all Dodge station wagon models accounted for a total of 51,600 sales, and in 1968 that figure had fallen to 50,000; whereas Plymouth built 91,984 wagons in 1960 and 95,420 in 1968. Full-size Fury models were offered throughout the decade, but compact Valiant wagon model production ceased in 1967, and Plymouth Belvedere intermediate-size wagon models were only introduced in 1965. The Dodge equivalent in the intermediate size was the Coronet.

Meanwhile, the two major surviving independent automakers continued to try to compete, and meet the unique needs of station wagon buyers by offering features not found in models produced by the big three.

By 1968, American Motors was again fighting to maintain market share. Although a serious competitor, by 1967, it was the last of the big independents in America. Sales had climbed steadily since its formation in 1954, but would peak in 1963 at a lofty production total of

While Plymouth continued with huge fins for 1960, equivalent Dodge models had much smaller fins, and a very different tail-end treatment, as seen on this Canadian Dodge Dart Pioneer, nine-passenger wagon, powered by a 318cu in (5.2L) V8. (Author's collection)

428,364 units. Sales declined after that, with a decade low in 1967 of just 237,785 cars, before rebounding to 239,937 units as the decade closed in 1969.

That didn't deter AMC from purchasing Kaiser Jeep in 1970, however. Although Jeep built the Wagoneer – which had appeared in 1963 – this large, 184-inch (467cm) long, 3600lb (1633kg) 4x4 vehicle was really a sport-utility model rather than a station wagon, as was the International Harvester Travellall, and smaller Scout Traveltop and Traveler.

Meanwhile, over at Studebaker, the situation was much worse. The Lark had initially been a smash hit, but competition from the Big Three and production and labour woes were continuing to grow.

Designer Brooks Stevens came up with some slick proposals for the 1964 to 1967 models, but in November 1963 was told to simply rework the existing Lark.

It was planned to close down South Bend, with all future car production out of Hamilton, Ontario. In 1964, the sporty Studebaker Hawk came to an end, just as the sexy Raymond Lowey Avanti coupe had. A corporate, as well as public lack of interest in Studebaker cars resulted in production being halted in Hamilton in 1966, and the company then concentrated on its more profitable divisions.

DODGE 330 9-PASSENGER WAG

DODGE 440 9-PASSENGER WAG

In 1963, the freshly restyled, American-built Dodge Dart was the equivalent compact of the sister division Plymouth Valiant, but in Canada the Dodge Dart was the full-size model with 84.4cu ft (2.4m) of cargo space and a cargo deck that was 9.8 feet (3m) long with the second seat folded and tailgate down. (Author's collection)

American Motors began the decade with an extensive line-up of intermediate and compact station wagons, including the luxury Ambassador, Rambler 6 and Rebel V8, as well as the basic, L-head 195.6cu in (3.2L) six-cylinder, reintroduced Rambler American. (Author's collection)

In 1968, American Motors offered three different wagon models, all with additional trim levels. The AMC Rebel and top-of-the-line Ambassador wagons shared a bodyshell, and differed only in grille, trim and lights, as well as standard equipment, available options, and powertrains. On the Rebel 550 and 770, and Ambassador and Ambassador DPL wagons, there was a choice of side opening or drop-down tailgate, but not both. Maximum cargo space on each was 94cu ft (2.7cu m). (Author's collection)

By 1968, the Rambler American was nearing the end of the line (all-new in 1964, and the first AMC built under the auspices of stylist Dick Teague.) The 4-door American 440 was powered by a small six, or you could order the optional, heftier 232cu in (3.8L) six-cylinder, or opt for one of two 292cu in (4.8L) V8s. Cargo space on this 106-inch (269cm) wheelbase wagon was a calculated 66cu ft (1.9cu m). (Author's collection)

Studebaker introduced a restyled, available-in-four-door-only station wagon version in 1963, known as the Wagonaire, and advertised as "… a stylish family car, a functional wagon, and a fun-filled convertible." It had some unique standard features, such as a sliding rear roof, handy tailgate, and a fold-down step. There was the choice of a 112hp Skybolt six or a 259cu in (4.2L) V8. A fixed-roof, stripped version of the station wagon was offered in mid-1963, known as the Lark. (Author's collection)

The Hamilton, Ontario, Canada-built 1966 Studebaker was the end of the line for this once-proud marque. Production ceased, despite the factory still turning a profit. Little had changed over the four years in production of the 113-inch (287cm) wheelbase wagon, other than a mild re-styling of the front end, side trim, and the expected industry updates. The biggest change was under the hood where the old Studebaker V8 had been replaced by a Chevrolet 283cu in (4.6L) V8. (Author's collection)

www.veloce.com/www.veloce.co.uk
Details of all books • New book news • Special offers

1970-1975: Practicality & change

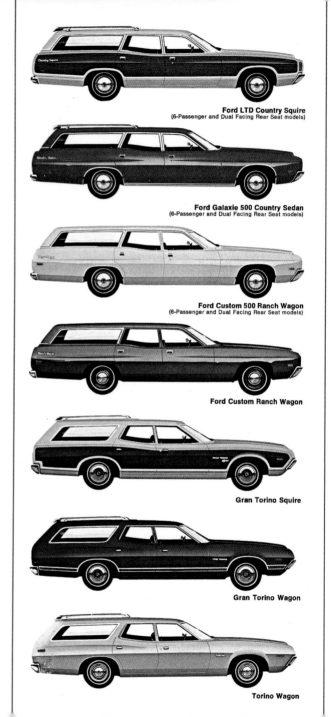

Ford LTD Country Squire
(6-Passenger and Dual Facing Rear Seat models)

Ford Galaxie 500 Country Sedan
(6-Passenger and Dual Facing Rear Seat models)

Ford Custom 500 Ranch Wagon
(6-Passenger and Dual Facing Rear Seat models)

Ford Custom Ranch Wagon

Gran Torino Squire

Gran Torino Wagon

Torino Wagon

By 1970 the station wagon had become a symbol of a successful, middle class American lifestyle. A home in suburbia and a station wagon in the double car garage, told the neighbors you were an 'up and comer.'

Yet, between 1970 and 1975 tremendous changes took place in the auto industry, and more importantly in American life.

Although high fuel consumption had been a concern of many in the past, the situation was quickly brought to a head, when the first OPEC-induced shortages began causing long line-ups at the gasoline pumps. It was all too common to see the closing of filling stations, and cardboard signs soon covered the rocketing high price fuel boards with a scrawled 'No Gas' sign. This became a common site at gas stations across North America – although more so in the US, than Canada.

This was something Americans had never felt before, and it soon led to fights, shootings and deaths at open gas stations during the most severe shortages. The deaths soon became national news stories which further 'fueled' the situation.

As a result, the American car manufacturers all started to 'downsize.' Everything was made smaller, lighter, and more fuel efficient. For example, Ford was

Ford called itself the 'Wagonmaster,' and in 1972 continued to offer an extensive line of full-size and intermediate station wagons. (Author's collection)

Special options on this full-size 1974 AMC Matador wagon included a luggage rack, tailgate air deflector, imitation wood-grain panels, a third seat with seatbelts, a rear cargo mat, and a power-lift rear window. A standard feature was the two-way tailgate for easy loading to fill the 99.1cu ft (2.8cu m) of cargo space. A handling package was also available which included heavy-duty springs and shock absorbers, plus a rear sway bar. (Author's collection)

The AMC Ambassador was the long-time, top-of-the-line model in the company's range, and in 1974 also. Standard features included air conditioning, an automatic transmission, 304cu in (5.0L) V8, power-operated steering and brakes, a light and visibility package, all-tinted glass, and much more. (Author's collection)

AMC preferred the term 'Hornet Sportabout' to station wagon. AMC wagon interiors could be ordered in either a very practical 'Venetian' custom fabric and vinyl, or luxurious 'Tru-Knit' vinyl in a choice of five fabric colors, depending on your preference back in 1974. (Author's collection)

one of the first to respond by introducing its 'new' Mustang in 1974. By the mid-1970s long gone were the high performance Shelby models, 428s, Mach 1s, etc. in favour of a Mustang with a standard four-cylinder model built on a Pinto platform.

Poor gas mileage in an era of quickly escalating gas prices hit North Americans in the place it hurt most – their pocket books. Cheap gas soon became a memory as the price per gallon rose daily.

The other major factor in the strangling of horsepower was the new pollution controls, upcoming government regulated fuel mileage averages, and an increase in safety regulations, all being imposed by the US government.

A quick fix for passing crash tests were bigger bumpers. American cars virtually overnight got heavier, slower and less maneuverable.

And, although styling remained very important, traditional designs and styling cues were constantly being reinvented or updated, to meet the changing times.

Still, the station wagon did have its practical functions and these characteristics were stressed even more by the mid-1970s, as the 'muscle car' era disappeared virtually overnight in 1973. Certainly there were still large, powerful cubic inch V8s offered, but the horsepower rating was declining fast. The reduction in horsepower was also a way of improving fuel consumption. Gas consumption became a major issue for American car manufacturers – albeit for all car builders around the world in the mid-seventies; although, the popularity of the American V8 and lack of four-cylinder models in the American car line-ups was highly conspicuous.

Downsizing would dramatically affect the model ranges, and the number of wagons offered was further reduced most often in favour of the lighter, less costly and easier to tool-up hatchbacks that were quickly growing in popularity.

Thus, the station wagons of the early seventies (1970 – 1973) were far different from the wagons built in 1974 and 1975. Those station wagons built during the

Ford bragged that the Pinto MPG (miles per gallon) Wagon came with all Pinto standard equipment, plus an EPA rating of 34mpg on the highway, and 23mpg in the city. Pictured is an MPG with the 'Squire' Option and white sidewall tires. (Author's collection)

The Canadian Pontiac Astre provided Pontiac-Olds dealers with a model to compete with the smaller imports, as well as GM's own Chevrolet Vega. Whereas roof racks were virtually a standard fixture for family vacations in the 1950s, by the 1970s, few Americans put no more on the roof of their car than possibly a canoe in the summer, or the family's skis in winter. Still, despite the extra wind noise and limited use, people liked the added style of a roof rack. (Author's collection)

The Chevrolet Vega was a popular little station wagon until reliability of the 90hp, 140cu in (2.3L) engine came into question, and brought a quick demise to GM's first real venture in the small car field. Despite this and other setbacks, Chevrolet saw itself as the make of 'America's car,' and promoted itself with the popular jingle "Baseball, hot dogs, apple pie and Chevrolet ..." Traditional wagon offerings continued in 1974 with mild face-lifts and model name changes to the intermediate-sized Chevelle Malibu Classic Estate, Malibu Classic and Malibu and full-size Caprice Estate, Caprice, Impala and Bel Air. (Author's collection)

Building a better way to see the U.S.A.   Chevrolet

last half of the 1970s were either mere facsimiles of once powerful V8 models, or awkwardly redesigned stopgap models until all-new designs could be introduced.

Yet, there were some fuel efficient American wagons built between 1970-1975 in the form of the Chevrolet Vega, Ford Pinto and the AMC Pacer. Chrysler offered some small wagons also, but these were mostly Mitsubishi-based models rather than American designs. The Mitsubishi, Dodge-badged,

The all-family Escape Machine 1970 Oldsmobile Vista-Cruiser

The full-size, unique, 121-inch (307cm) wheelbase 1970 Oldsmobile Vista Cruiser was more stylish and far better-selling (10,758 units in two-seat form, and 23,336 more units in three-seat form) than the smaller Cutlass (7680 units in V8 form and just 85 units in six-cylinder guise). Standard power unit in the Vista Cruiser was the 250hp, 350cu in (5.7L) V8. Popular optional equipment included a transmission oil cooler, a roof luggage rack, heavy-duty shock absorbers, and a rear air deflector. (Courtesy Thomas McPherson)

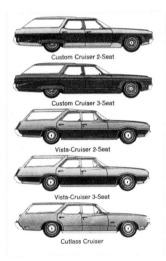

Custom Cruiser 2-Seat

Custom Cruiser 3-Seat

Vista-Cruiser 2-Seat

Vista-Cruiser 3-Seat

Cutlass Cruiser

For 1971, Oldsmobile introduced its 127-inch (323cm) wheelbase Custom Cruiser "… totally new luxury, full-size wagon with disappearing tailgate!" although this, the 'Glide-Away Tailgate,' would prove to be a problem. Other 1971 wagons included the 11-window Vista-Cruiser with its 10cu ft (0.283cu m) of cargo space accessed via a 'Drop-or-Swing Tailgate,' and the Cutlass Cruiser that featured under floor storage. (Author's collection)

Colt line appeared in 1971, including a station wagon version. (Some of the Rootes-based wagon models did arrive in North America, and were sold as Plymouth models. The Plymouth Cricket was offered until 1973.) In 1974 the better selling, more reliable Mitsubishi Colt models bearing the Plymouth nameplate took over.

GM redesigned its full-size wagons in 1971 following the round-sided styling trend known as 'tumblehome,' which the industry soon realized was more prone to rust in the tucked-under fenders and rockers. GM also pioneered a new rear tailgate that saw the glass disappear into the roof and the tailgate into the body. Dirt tended to get into the openings, which fouled the power option, while the manual pulling out of the tailgate proved to be both difficult and heavy. The design was eventually abandoned.

Meanwhile, Ford continued its dominance of the station wagon market. Outselling every wagon in the

Chrysler and Plymouth continued to offer a full line of wagons in 1973 – including the British-based, sub-compact Plymouth Cricket. The full-size Plymouth wagon pictured is the Fury Sport Suburban. (Author's collection)

country – big or small, was the Ford Pinto wagon. This was the best selling station wagon in the first half of the 1970s. It was powered by a 2.3L, 2V, four-cylinder engine and fitted with a standard four-speed transmission. A popular option with Americans was the three-speed automatic transmission. In these fuel shortage times, the Pinto station wagon with its four-speed transmission and a 3.18 axle ration and a catalytic converter squeezed out an EPA (Environmental Protection Agency) rating of 34mpg highway, and 23mpg city. Like all American cars the Pinto Wagon was available with a long list of options including, air conditioning, full wheel discs, whitewall

Town & Country Station Wagon

Extra care in engineering
it makes a difference. 29

In 1973, the full-size, top-of-the-line was the Chrysler Town & Country Wagon, which still harked back to the bygone 'Woody' era in both name and imitation wood-grain panels. (Author's collection)

tires, stereo upgrades and a traditional 'Squire' wood treatment.

While subcompact station wagons had become more popular as the decade continued, due chiefly to the fuel crisis, the American manufacturers continued to offer compact, intermediate and full-size wagons. Although sales had decreased somewhat, there was still a substantial demand for larger station wagons, for traditional buyers who found the size far more practical for use in their daily lives; but the golden era was over.

The Station Wagon today

Old wagons

For years collectors tended to ignore old station wagons, as vehicles not worth the cost of restoration. Those who had once owned old station wagons were seen as the buttoned-down-collar, family man, or the mother, who transported the kids to school, traveled to the shopping malls, and hauled home bags of food from the grocery store each week.

This 1966, 170-Series Dodge Dart wagon was originally delivered with a 273.cu in (4.5L) V8 and equipped with only a few options, but is now fitted with a larger, high performance, 360cu in (5.9L) V8 with a quick shift transmission, heavy-duty sway bars front and rear, four gas shocks with power steering and power disc brakes added, and a stainless steel dual exhaust. Added creature comforts consist of air conditioning, six-way power bucket seats, a custom centre console with cup holders and extra power ports, tinted glass, and the entire interior recovered in a cloth and vinyl custom design – yet this Dart looks stock from a distance! (Courtesy Fred Dol)

Like many wagons today, this 1957 Pontiac Chieftain Station Wagon has undergone numerous changes and updates to increase driving pleasure, yet the original essence of this wagon has not been lost, and the make is instantly recognizable. Power brakes, a dual master cylinder, more comfortable seats and seatbelts, air conditioning, new shocks, larger wheels and tires, and a slightly more modern, bigger V8 all help make older station wagons fit better into today's traffic conditions. (Courtesy Dave Cleveland)

Other station wagons do become full, radical customs. Modifications can include not only drivetrain, comfort and convenience changes, but also chopped tops, custom grilles and lights, etc, as seen on this 1956 Chevrolet. (Author's collection)

Some wagons are also modified to full show circuit guise, such as this 1951 Nash Rambler Model 151. Full customizing can mean that the original make and model can be identified by only the most knowledgeable enthusiasts. (Author's collection)

Certainly, the family or small businessman's station wagon saw yeoman's duty to the point where their vehicles were worked literally to death, and usually ended-up in a junkyard to be parted-out or crushed. As a result, only a relatively small percentage of the vast numbers of station wagons built from 1950 – 1975 survive today.

Of those that have endured the decades of use, many have been upgraded or customized, either to add pizzazz and power to these domestic workhorses, or to avoid the same image as the original owners.

Thus, at car shows and cruises in North America today, one rarely finds a fully restored or original example. Even then, with the emphasis on vehicle safety, the traveling of great distances to attend car shows in other states, and vehicle personalization, fewer and fewer of the surviving station wagons from this era are restored to original condition.

Another more practical reason for this is the disappearance of replacement wagon parts.

(Many station wagons over the ensuing decades have been stripped of basic parts, to restore more collectible convertibles and hardtops before being crushed.)

The most common changes made to older station wagons today by collectors include engine swaps – particularly six-cylinder models to V8 – the fitting of modern mag-style wheels with radial or low-profile tires, the changing to disc brakes and addition of dual braking systems, the installation of the latest sound systems, removing the front bench-seat in favour of power-operated bucket seats, and, making numerous suspension changes in order to improve handling and driving enjoyment.

Chrome and trim – especially on fifties and early sixties station wagons – is extremely difficult to find, and very expensive to replace or re-plate, due to the vastness of the bumpers, grilles, etc. and lavish amount of adornment.

As a result, shortcuts are often taken, such as

As a result, shortcuts are often taken, such as the painting of chrome; fitting newer trim, bumpers or aftermarket custom grilles; or by simply leaving some pieces off.

The paint colors, originally available from the car manufacturers, ranged from spectacular three-tones, to drab, lackluster pastels, all white or simply black. Today many owners choose to re-spray their station wagons in more modern colors.

These modified station wagons or mild customs may not have survived if it had not been for these collectors. Many would have been crushed for scrap metal, or become future donor cars. In most cases the basic originality of these station wagons has been maintained, and can be enjoyed by all enthusiasts.

Yet, a very original station wagon will always be appreciated.

New wagons

By the last half of the 1970s, North Americans had experienced the reality of the first oil crisis, and growing government concern over poor fuel economy. American car manufacturers were forced to downsize. No longer would the adage of 'bigger is better' be acceptable.

Along with downsizing was the growing world-wide trend toward front-wheel-drive, from traditional rear-wheel-drive models. Building smaller and lighter vehicles, meant more fuel-efficient four- and six-cylinder

Since the late 1970s, station wagons continued to be introduced. No longer an expected staple in every model line-up, they are more niche models, produced in order to fulfill a perceived need in a particular market. (2002 Ford Taurus wagon pictured: courtesy Ford Motor Company)

Neither Ford nor GM replied with a station wagon to compete head-on with the DaimlerChrysler Dodger Magnum (pictured) in 2005. The Magnum was dropped in 2009. (Courtesy DaimlerChrysler)

engines could be fitted, to improve the mandated corporate fuel economy average.

American cars were changing, and the role of the traditional station wagon was changing too. Although station wagons continued to be offered throughout American car line-ups, more and more families and small businesses were looking for alternatives, and found them in the bigger, extended cab pickup trucks and vans, still being offered by the American manufacturers.

The rebirth in popularity of the two-box design in America in the 1980s, first came in the form of 'station wagons on steroids' with the All-Wheel Drive and 4X4s adding a new dimension in functionality. These variations had two or three rows of seats, and a traditional American station wagon tailgate. While the Jeep Wagoneer and International Harvester, Travelall,

had pioneered this type of vehicle in the 1960s, it wasn't until the 1980s that the concept really caught on in North America.

Yet, despite the huge impact SUVs and Crossovers have had on the station wagon market, it was the minivan that initially stole most of the sales away from the traditional station wagon.

Although small vans had been around for decades, it was the Plymouth Voyager and Dodge Caravan new generation of minivans that appeared in 1984, that became the modern mode of family transportation. The minivan in America would soon become the new station wagon. Its introduction, and subsequent market domination, virtually eliminated the need for the traditional station wagon in many buyers' minds.

North Americans embraced the idea, and in its first

year just over 100,000 were sold, but in 1985 that figure would jump to over 210,000 units and continue to climb, approaching nearly 500,000 Chrysler-built minivans in 1990.

Still, driving a minivan or SUV was different than driving a station wagon. Some buyers disliked front-wheel-drive, while others did not like sitting as far forward or as high. The handling and the ride qualities of these vehicles were also obviously different, and almost truck-like in some cases. Traditional station wagon owners wanted the driving attributes of a car, as well as practicality.

As a result, American manufacturers continued to offer station wagons – but designed to fill niche markets. And, as those small markets faded in and out, so did the station wagon models.

Over the past twenty years American attempts to re-introduce the station wagon have met with minimal to moderate short-term success.

DaimlerChrysler introduced its full-size Dodge Magnum in 2005, but there was no equivalent model from either General Motors or Ford. Interestingly, although it had all the looks and station wagon DNA, Chrysler refused to call it a station wagon or even 'sportwagon'.

Today, despite the station wagon's highly functional body style, that is so well suited to North American needs, few are even considered. A new 'golden age' of the traditional station wagon in North America which will likely never return.

Variations on a theme

Throughout the 1950s and into the 1970s, various manufacturers tried to bring to the market the many virtues appreciated by station wagon owners, in a more traditional car design, and less utilitarian-looking in appearance.

Following WWII, many of the smaller independent manufacturers either couldn't afford to spend the development money to compete in the station wagon market, or chose to concentrate mainly on higher demand, production sedans. This was also the transition period for station wagon design and construction. Traditional, up-market 'woody' station wagons faded from the scene in favour of the less expensive to build, and higher volume, all-metal models.

With more roads and interstate highways for driving longer distances, sleeping in your car or station wagon appealed to many Americans, as an inexpensive way to see the country.

Nash had built 'Woody' station wagons prior to WWII, but with its Airflyte sedans featuring folding seats for bed-like comfort, and a large trunk, the firm felt these cars were a good alternative to the additional cost of developing a station wagon version. (Courtesy Andrew Mort)

The dual 'airliner' reclining seats adjusted to five positions, including day-bed level or "... Your own private Sleeping Car ..." complete with twin beds. Nash offered as an option firstly, a feather-filled mattress, and later, air mattresses for comfortable overnight sleeping for sportsmen and vacationers. (Courtesy Andrew Mort)

To make overnight sleeping in your Nash even more comfortable, there were optional slip-on insect screens, which were, "... available at a slight extra cost." (Courtesy Andrew Mort)

As well as a stylish interior created by Madame Helene Rother of Paris, the Nash Airflyte sedans were totally practical from a traveller's point-of-view. Niceties included a handy storage drawer for personal items built into the dash. (Courtesy Andrew Mort)

Nash had been a major auto manufacturer since 1916, and in 1941 was the first American automaker to introduce unibody construction in mass-produced, low priced cars.

Nash was the largest and most successful independent automaker following WWII, and the new station wagon-like 1949 Nash Ambassador, and 600 Airflyte sedans soon became known for turning into a bedroom on wheels. With its folding seats and optional bedroom-like options, Nash stressed the fact that it was "... the 'travelingist' car in the world – specifically designed to make your travel dreams come true. No worry about sleeping accommodations; ready anytime."

As for cargo space; the Nash trunk was advertised as "... holds enough baggage for a family of six on a cross-country trip."

Nash continued to offer its sleeping option and boast of its generous trunk space right-up to its disappearance as a make in 1957. Some of the Nash-based Hudson models also offered this feature following the formation of AMC in 1954. Although the sedan sleepers proved popular and were offered through the 1950s, Nash did see the need for a traditional station wagon in its line-up as early as 1951.

Independent automaker Kaiser-Frazer also offered a very viable alternative to the traditional station wagon.

Following WWII, industrialist Henry J Kaiser joined Graham-Paige executive Joseph Frazer and formed a new car company to build cars under their names, styled by famed designer Howard 'Dutch' Darrin. This 1951 Frazer Vagabond was marketed as a "Smart successor to the station wagon – converts in 10 seconds from roomy, comfortable sedan to spacious carrier … for sports or business use." (Author's collection)

Frazer Vagabond

Smart successor to the station wagon—converts in 10 seconds from roomy, comfortable sedan to a spacious carrier...for sports or business use.

The Kaiser Traveler and more luxurious Frazer Vagabond models first appeared in 1949. Originally these were standard four-door sedans, that required about two hundred changes to become the utility car that Henry Kaiser first suggested. As well as expected changes to create a hatch, tailgate and rear deck, the left rear door was welded shut and the spare tire mounted vertically. Kaiser-Frazer promoted these utility vehicles to farmers, carpenters, sportsmen and even funeral homes.

In 1951 the new two-door sedan Kaiser was also offered as a Traveler model.

Despite the fact the Traveler and Vagabond models

were less than $100US more than a regular sedan, and considerably less than the average station wagon, these hatchback alternatives were not a huge sales success in the long run. Incidentally, Chrysler had offered similar, yet less versatile Carry-All models from 1949 – 1951. These too sold poorly.

In the 1949 – 1950 calendar year one-quarter of the K-F sales were Traveler or Vagabond models, but that volume percentage dwindled dramatically over the next year, to less than one thousand Travelers in its final model year in 1953. Still, the Kaiser Traveler and Frazer Vagabond models in three-door and four-door form were

"The World's Most Useful Car" – even in two-door form – was how Kaiser described its Traveler, in a 1951 model line-up brochure. Featuring a 'durable vinyl' interior, it was an easy conversion from sedan to carrier without tools. The brochure added "The best answer on wheels for florists, salesmen, repairmen – everyone who needs a car to carry bulky equipment for business and a smart sedan for family use." (Author's collection)

the American predecessor of the popular hatchbacks, that would eventually be offered by all of the domestic brands during the 1970s.

As already noted, the hatchback alternative to the traditional station wagon began to appear in showrooms across America in the late 1960s. The hatchback appeared to have all the versatility of a station wagon, yet featured far more stylish and sportier lines. The four major American car manufacturers embraced the idea and soon there were hatchbacks in every model line-up (except Lincoln and Cadillac, which in most cases were the larger full-size models). Interestingly, it was a concept that ultimately proved to be far more popular in Canada per capita, than in the US.

While there was never a full-size American hatchback model offered, this body style was commonly seen throughout the compact and sub-compact line-ups, and on a few intermediate-sized cars.

The first American hatchbacks to appear were developed on the new wave of American sub-compact models. Two of the most stylish General Motors hatchbacks offered were the Chevy Vega and Pontiac Astre (an added Canadian-only model).

The Vega and Astre were also offered in two-door sedan, panel van and station wagon models.

The sleek-looking hatchbacks came in various forms including GT guise with the ultimate hatchback Vega being the usually black and gold Cosworth model.

Pontiac brochures tried to attract buyers through scenarios such as "It looks like a little Pontiac Astre coupe. Until you're standing on the sidewalk with an armful of packages and one antique lamp. That's when you open the hatch, fold down the rear seat and discover your Astre isn't so little inside. With the rear seat folded you've got 66 inches (168cm) of cargo length, 18.9cu ft (0.54cu m) to pack and carry all the things that just wouldn't fit in most small economy cars." (Author's collection)

The Gremlin – an AMC Hornet two-door sedan with the trunk cut-off – would have benefited from a folding tailgate for easier access. Despite this omission, it proved popular, however, partly due to its 'big car' ride and feel; standard six-cylinder power and top speed of 95mph (153km/h). AMC also offered the Hornet in wagon and hatchback forms to broaden appeal. (Author's collection)

Another hot hatchback was the Monza which was introduced in 1975 with V8 power.

Over the ensuing years Chevrolet would offer hatchback versions in its Chevette, Monza, Citation, Cavalier, Nova and even its sporty Camaro. In many cases station wagon versions were offered in some of these models as the hatchbacks were moving away from practical use with more emphasis on performance.

Although less sporty-looking, Ford's Pinto hatchback offered more station wagon-like features, without the sensibleness of its alternative wagon version.

Meanwhile, AMC developed its sub-compact car, based on its popular compact Hornet model. It was a brilliant move that saved millions in development money, while also providing dealers with a new model to compete within this new market. The single body style Gremlin was more wagon-like in profile than most hatchbacks and marketed with a variety of options, and a high level of standard equipment, which included air conditioning.

Another hatchback AMC offered was in its compact Hornet line. Sporty, as well as practical, the Hornet Hatchback proved immensely popular. Yet, AMC continued to develop and offer station wagons in its compact and intermediate-size line-ups.

The hatchback's ultimate fall from grace was due to criticisms regarding noise, vibration and rattles. There were also difficulties associated with opening the rear hatch in wet and snowy weather, and the gradual failure of the gas struts required for lifting and holding the hatch open. Still, it would be a concept repeatedly revisited by car makers around the world, just as has been the case with station wagons. A wide variety of model lines from both foreign and American manufacturers have continued to offer hatchbacks. Most have appeared and then disappeared only to re-appear time and again – as have station wagons; but seldom as a market leader.

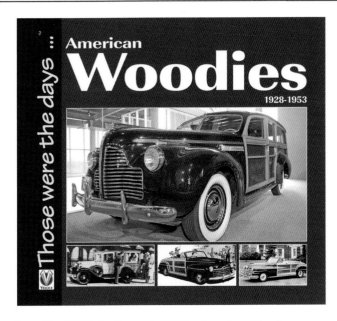

From the 1920s to the early 1950s, American Woodies came in a variety of models, including station wagons, convertibles, and sedans. Whereas the station wagons were built for functionality, Woodie sedans and convertibles were constructed purely for style.

£14.99*
ISBN 978-1-845842-69-7

Covers the attempts made by major makes such as Kaiser-Nash, Willys, Packard, Studebaker, Tucker, Nash and Hudson to compete with the 'Big Three' in postwar America.

£14.99*
ISBN 978-1-845842-39-3

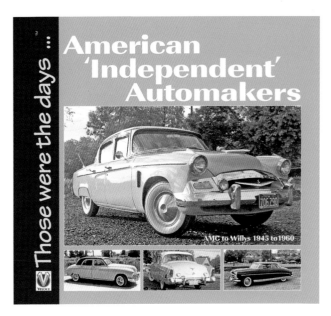

For more info on Veloce titles, visit our website at www.veloce.co.uk • email info@veloce.co.uk • tel +44(0)1305 260068
* prices subject to change • p&p extra

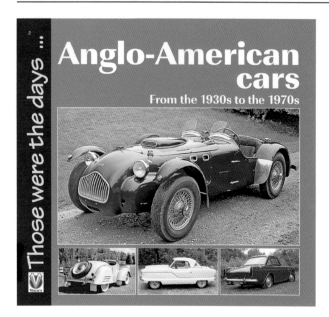

Covers British cars powered by American engines, and American cars fitted with British powerplants, all built from the 1930s to the 1970s.

£14.99*
ISBN 978-1-845842-33-8

Highlighting the work of hundreds of small coachbuilders, and illustrated with 100 rare and previously unpublished photographs this book is a tribute to the skills of the people who built these amazing wooden wonders

.

£12.99 *
ISBN 978-1-845841-69-0

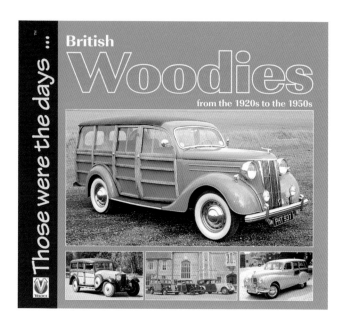

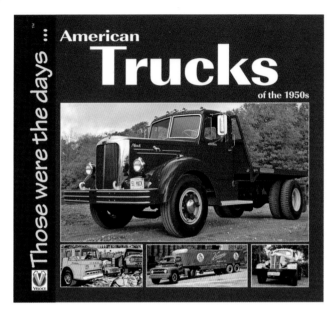

This highly visual study examines the important role of trucking in the growth of North America in the 1950s, and the essential part it played in the industrial growth of the US and Canada.

£14.99*
ISBN 978-1-845842-27-7

This highly visual study examines the important role of trucking in the 1960s, when stiff competition resulted in failures and mergers.

£14.99*
ISBN 978-1-845842-28-4

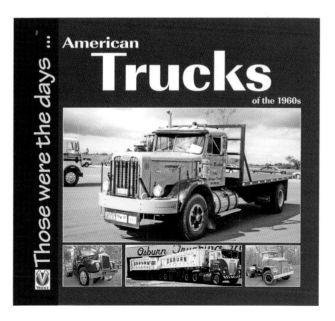

Index